GYMNASTICS

A TRUE BOOK

by

Christin Ditchfield

Children's Press®
A Division of Grolier Publishing

New York London Hong Kong Sydney
Danbury, Connecticut

A gymnast being spotted on the uneven bars

Reading Consultant
Linda Cornwell
*Coordinator of School Quality
and Professional Improvement
Indiana State Teachers
Association*

Author's Dedication
*For Stephanie, who did
cartwheels everywhere she
went when she was little.*

*The photo on the cover
shows gymnast Betty Okino
on the beam. The photo on
the title page shows a young
gymnast practicing on the
pommel horse.*

**Visit Children's Press® on the
Internet at:
http://publishing.grolier.com**

Library of Congress Cataloging-in-Publication Data

Ditchfield, Christin.
    Gymnastics / by Christin Ditchfield.
        p.   cm. — (A true book)
    Includes bibliographical references (p.   ) and index.
    Summary: Describes the history, equipment, events, and scoring of
gymnastics.
    ISBN 0-516-21063-7 (lib.bdg.)   0-516-27026-5 (pbk.)
    1. Gymnastics Juvenile literature. [1. Gymnastics.] I. Title.
II. Series.
GV461.3.D58   2000
796.44—dc21   99-28208
                                                                                    CIP
                                                                                    AC

GROLIER
PUBLISHING

Contents

Olga Korbut during the 1972 Olympics

The Girl who Smiled

The 1972 Olympic Games were about to start. One of the girls on the Soviet Union's gymnastics team got hurt. Olga Korbut was chosen to take the injured girl's place. Olga was seventeen years old, but she looked much younger. She was only 4 feet, 11 inches (150 cm) tall. No one had ever heard of Olga. No one expected her to win a medal. But she did!

In fact, Olga Korbut won a total of four medals at the Munich Olympics—three gold and one silver. She also changed the sport of gymnastics forever.

At that time, women's gymnastics was more like ballet or some other kind of dancing. The gymnasts performed their routines slowly and gracefully.

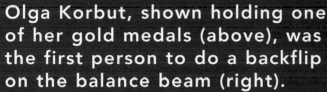

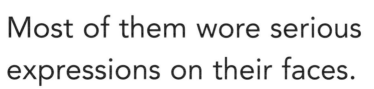
Olga Korbut, shown holding one of her gold medals (above), was the first person to do a backflip on the balance beam (right).

Most of them wore serious expressions on their faces.

Olga, however, was quick and lively. She amazed the crowds—and the other gymnasts—with her daring moves.

Olga was the first person to do a backflip on the balance beam—and she was the first gymnast to smile at the audience while she performed.

Millions of people watched Olga on television. They liked her energy and her happy, friendly personality. Many boys and girls who were watching decided that they wanted to be gymnasts too. Within the next few years, many more gymnastics

People loved watching Olga perform.

clubs and training centers were opened to teach them.

Gymnastics was suddenly one of the most popular sports in the world. And all because of the girl who smiled.

Long Ago

The sport of gymnastics is more than two thousand years old! It was invented by the people of ancient Greece. The Greeks believed that physical exercise was an important part of health and education. They built a gymnasium in every major city so

that the citizens could do
these exercises regularly.

The ancient Romans used
gymnastics to train their sol-
diers and keep them ready for

Acrobats doing gymnastics in the 1700s

battle. In the Middle Ages, circus performers entertained crowds with some of the same acrobatic skills that gymnasts perform today.

A German schoolteacher named Friedrich Jahn opened the first modern gymnastics center in the early 1800s. Jahn taught his students about the

Friedrich Jahn

importance of exercise for good health. He also invented special equipment to help them—including the parallel bars and the pommel horse. His teachings soon spread all over the world. Jahn became known as the Father of Modern Gymnastics.

The first modern Olympic Games were held in 1896 in Athens, Greece. Back then, only men competed in the Olympics. Gymnastics was one

Gymnasts on the rings (left) and parallel bars (below) during the 1896 Olympic Games

of the first sports to be included in the competition.

The events that were called "gymnastics" included not only those performed today (horizontal bar, parallel bars, pommel horse, rings, and vault), but also rope-climbing, club-swinging, pole-vaulting, and wrestling.

Women were not allowed to compete in gymnastics in the Olympics until 1928. Even then, there was only one

Team combined exercise was the first women's gymnastic event in the Olympics.

event for women—team combined exercise—and it was actually closer to dancing than what we think of today as gymnastics.

Many things have changed since then.

The Apparatus

A piece of equipment used in a gymnastics competition is called an apparatus.

Women perform on the vaulting horse (or vault), the balance beam, the uneven parallel bars, and the floor (a large square mat). Men perform on the vault, the pommel horse, the rings, the horizontal bar, the parallel bars, and the floor.

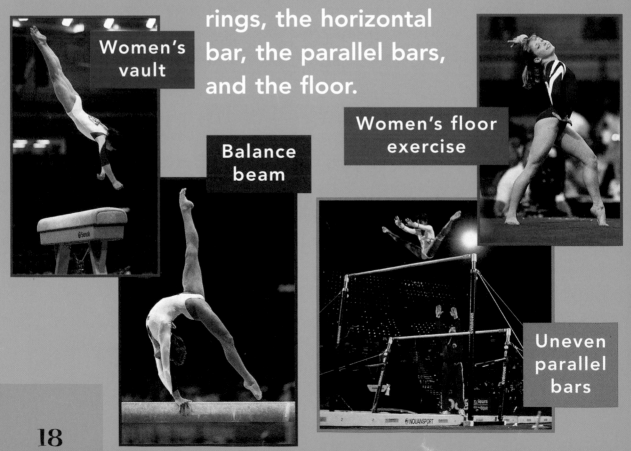

Women's vault

Balance beam

Women's floor exercise

Uneven parallel bars

For some apparatus, the gymnast is assisted by a "spotter"— a partner or coach who stands nearby, ready to give the gymnast a lift up to the equipment or catch a gymnast who falls.

Rings

Men's vault

Horizontal bar

Parallel bars

Pommel horse

Men's floor exercise

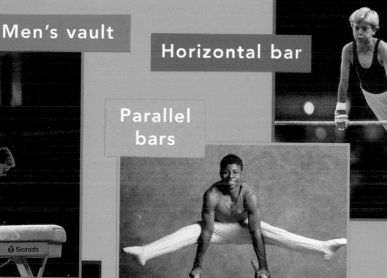

The Events

Today there are many gymnastics competitions. There are junior competitions for beginners and senior competitions for advanced gymnasts. There are college competitions and national competitions. And then there are international competitions—such as the Olympic Games, the

Gymnastics meets take place in gymnasiums or arenas.

Pan-American Games, and the Goodwill Games.

These competitions (called meets) take place in gymnasiums or arenas. Men and women compete separately.

In any gymnastics competition, the gymnasts must
perform two types of routines:
compulsory and optional. A
compulsory routine is an
assigned routine that must be
performed by every gymnast

in exactly the same way. This type of routine gives the judges a way of directly comparing the skills of all the gymnasts.

In an optional routine, the gymnast gets to decide which movements to do. Sometimes a gymnast will create his or her own move that no one has done before. The move is then named for the gymnast who invented it. Other gymnasts learn the move and add it to their own routines.

The Yurchenko vault, a vault done from a round-off handspring entry, is named for Soviet gymnast Natalia Yurchenko.

At a women's meet, the gymnasts compete in four events. The first event is the vault. The gymnast runs toward the vaulting horse and jumps on a springboard. Putting her hands on the horse for balance, she flips across its width. She may do a twist, somersault, or some other movement in the air before landing on her feet. It is important to "stick" her landing—to take no extra steps after she lands.

On the uneven bars, the gymnast leaps up and grabs onto one of the bars. The gymnast then swings back and forth from one bar to the other. At the same time, she performs difficult moves such as aerials, handstands, or splits. She must

A gymnast stays in constant motion while on the uneven bars.

perform the entire routine smoothly, without ever stopping.

The balance beam is a long wooden beam that is only 4 inches (10 cm) wide. On this apparatus, a gymnast must do cartwheels, handsprings, and flips—without falling off! The gymnast's goal is to move so gracefully and confidently that she gives the impression of performing on a floor rather than on a thin strip of wood.

Gymnasts strive to make the beam—a difficult event—look easy.

The women's floor exercise (left) and men's floor exercise (below)

In the floor exercise, the gymnast performs a tumbling routine on a large, square floor mat. For her optional routine, she chooses her own music and adds dance movements in between the flips, somersaults, and other tumbling moves.

Male gymnasts compete in six events. A few of them are similar to women's events. For instance, men do the floor exercise—but without music or dancelike moves. They also compete in

the vault, but male gymnasts vault over the length of the horse rather than the width.

The pommel horse looks a lot like the vaulting horse. It gets its name from the two handles on the top, called pom-mels. The gymnast supports himself by holding onto the pommels. He swings his legs in circles and from side to side across the horse. Sometimes his whole body weight is supported by one arm as he straddles the horse.

The pommel horse

The rings (above) and parallel bars (right) require tremendous upper-body strength.

One of the most difficult events is the rings. Two wooden rings hang from cables connected to the ceiling. The rings are more than 8 feet (2.4 m) above the floor. The gymnast leaps up and grabs the rings. Keeping them as still as possible, he performs handstands and other moves. It takes tremendous strength for a gymnast to hold himself up in the air through the whole routine.

On the parallel bars, the gymnast supports himself with his hands while performing handstands and other swinging stunts.

The last men's event is the horizontal bar. The gymnast flips and twists as he swings up, over, and around the bar. He does not come to a full stop until the routine is finished.

All the events, both men's and women's, require strength, flexibility, and balance.

Newer Events

In 1984, a new gymnastics competition was officially added to the Olympic Games. In this event, called rhythmic gymnastics, women gymnasts perform short routines set to music. The routines are done on the floor mat and involve ribbons, hoops, balls, clubs, or ropes. A gymnast

Rhythmic gymnastics with ribbon (top), a ball (above), and clubs (right)

is awarded points for the difficulty of her movements. She is also judged for the skill with

Trampoline gymnasts jump high in the air and perform single, double, triple, or twisting somersaults before landing back on the trampoline.

which she releases—and then catches—the equipment.

Trampoline gymnastics appeared for the first time in the Olympics at the 2000 Olympic Games in Sydney, Australia.

The Winners

The winner of a competition is decided by a group of judges who carefully watch each routine. They award points for skill and form. They give extra points for moves that are very difficult or very creative. The judges subtract points when a gymnast falls or makes a mistake—such

A judge holds up a score (above). At the 1976 Montreal Olympics, Rumanian gymnast Nadia Comaneci (right) became the first gymnast to score a perfect "10."

as skipping a compulsory move. The highest possible score is a "10."

Each judge gives the gymnast a score, and all the judges' scores are averaged together for a final score. A gymnast receives a final score for each apparatus. In an "all-around" competition, the

Golden Girls

At the Summer Olympics in 1984, Mary Lou Retton became the first American woman to win a gold medal in gymnastics. She also won two silver medals and two bronze medals! Mary Lou's style was strong and powerful. Her personality was bubbly and bright. Reporters called her "America's Sweetheart."

Mary Lou Retton

At the Atlanta Olympics in 1996, Amanda Borden, Amy Chow, Dominique Dawes, Jaycie Phelps, Shannon Miller, Dominique Moceanu, and Kerri Strug helped the United States win its first-ever gold medal in the team competition. They earned their

"The Magnificent Seven"

very own nickname—"The Magnificent Seven."

gymnast who has the best scores overall wins the meet.

In team competitions, the judges take the best five all-around scores of the team members. These are added together to get the total team score. The team with the highest score wins.

Gymnastics is not an easy sport. It takes years of practice and hard work to become a skilled gymnast. Many gymnasts move far away from their families to work with a special

coach at a professional train-ing center.

To be in good shape, gym-nasts have to be careful to eat healthy foods. They have to get enough rest. The gymnas-tics moves are dangerous, and sometimes athletes get hurt. There is no guarantee that they will win the medal they have worked so hard for. But when a gymnast feels the thrill of victory, it all seems worthwhile!

All the hard work seems worthwhile when a gymnast knows a routine has gone well.

To Find Out More

Here are some additional resources to help you learn more about gymnastics:

Books

Greenspan, Bud. **One Hundred Greatest Moments in Olympic History.** General Publishing Group, 1995.

Gutman, Dan. **Gymnastics.** Viking, 1996.

McSweeney, Sean and Chris Bunnett. **Gymnastics.** B.T. Batsford Ltd.,1993.

Readhead, Lloyd. T**he Fantastic Book of Gymnastics.** Copper Beach Books, 1997.

☀ Organizations and Online Sites

All About Gymnastics
http://member.aol.com/ msdaizy/sports3/gymnast. html

Lots of information about gymnastics, including history, fun facts, a glossary of gymnastics terms, and information on women's and men's events.

Fédération internationale de gymnastique
Rue des Oeuches 10
Case Postale 359
CH 2740 Moutier 1
Switzerland
http://www.worldsport. com/sports/gymnastics/ home.html

The FIG is the international governing body of the sport of gymnastics. Its website offers the latest news, results, pictures, and profiles of gymnasts and gymnastics.

Gymnastics Hall of Fame
227 Brooks Street
Oceanside, CA 92054

Exhibits on the world's most accomplished gymnasts.

USA Gymnastics
Pan American Plaza,
Suite 300
201 South Capitol Avenue
Indianapolis, IN 46225
http://www. usagymnastics.org

This is the national governing body for the sport of gymnastics in the United States. Its website has loads of information about gymnastics, including descriptions of events, schedules, and how the U.S. Olympic team gets chosen.

USOC Online
http://www.usoc.org

The website of the United States Olympic Committee includes everything you want to know about Olympic sports, past and present.

Important Words

acrobatic having to do with tumbling

aerial move in which a gymnast turns completely over in the air without touching the apparatus with his or her hands

dismount move a gymnast uses to get off an apparatus at the end of a routine

gymnasium building or room designed for indoor sports and exercise

routine set of movements a gymnast performs on an apparatus

somersault any movement in which a gymnast rotates in a complete circle in the air

spotter partner or coach who stands nearby during a routine to assist or support a gymnast

straddle to position the legs wide apart

Index

Meet the Author

Christin Ditchfield is the author of several books for Children's Press, including five True Books on the Summer Olympics. Her interviews with celebrity athletes have appeared in magazines all over the world. Ms. Ditchfield makes her home in Sarasota, Florida.